GW00976506

This book belongs to

BENJAMIN JAMES MᶜGLADE

05.07.09   CHRISTENING

FROM NANA - GODMOTHER

Copyright © 2003 Lion Hudson plc/
Tim Dowley & Peter Wyart
trading as Three's Company
All rights reserved.

Text and illustrations by Eira Reeves

Published 2003 by Candle Books
(a publishing imprint of Lion Hudson plc).
Reprinted 2004

ISBN 1 85985 471 0

Distributed in UK by
Marston Book Services Ltd, PO Box 269,
Abingdon, Oxon OX14 4YN

Distributed in the US by
Kregel Publications
P.O. Box 2607, Grand Rapids, Michigan 49501

ISBN 0 8254 7271 7

Worldwide co-edition organized and
produced by Lion Hudson plc,
Mayfield House, 256 Banbury Road,
Oxford, OX2 7DH, England.
·Tel: +44 (0) 1865 302750
Fax: +44 (0) 1865 302757
Email: coed@lionhudson.com
www.lionhudson.com

Printed in China

My Very First Bible

Eira Reeves

CANDLE
BOOKS

Contents

Abram leaves home

Long, long ago, in a far-off land called Ur,
there lived a man named Abram.
One day God spoke to him.

"I am going to give you a special land," God promised.
"Look up! Can you count the stars?
One day there will be more people in your family
than there are stars in the sky!"

So Abram packed his bags and loaded up his animals. Then he set out with his family to look for this special land. He believed God.

After many months,
Abram came at last to the land God had promised.
There he stayed with his wife, Sarah, and their son, Isaac.

Genesis 12:1–9, 21:1–7

God changed Abram's name to Abraham.
And God gave Abraham great flocks of sheep
and herds of camels.

Now Abraham's son, Isaac, had two sons,
Esau and Jacob. Esau was a hunter,
but Jacob, the younger son,
was very sneaky.

One day, Jacob went to his blind, old father,
and pretended to be Esau.
Isaac gave Jacob his special blessing, instead of Esau.

Esau was so angry that Jacob had to run away.
He went to a far country.

Genesis 25:19–34, 27:1–45

15

One night, as Jacob slept on a rock,
he dreamed he saw angels climbing
up and down stairs to heaven.
God promised him,
"I will always look after your family."

Genesis 28:10–22

Years later, Jacob came back to the Promised Land.
Jacob made up with his brother, Esau.
Now Jacob had a big family of twelve sons.

Jacob loved Joseph more than his older brothers.
Jacob gave him a special coat.
How wonderful he looked!

18

And how jealous Joseph's brothers were!
They were so angry that they took Joseph
and sold him to traders.
They told Jacob that Joseph was dead.
Jacob wept.

Genesis 37:1–36

19

Joseph had lots of adventures in Egypt.
First he was an army captain's slave,
then he was thrown into jail.
Finally Joseph was made top minister
to Pharaoh, the ruler of Egypt!

Genesis 38–41

One year, no rain fell in Egypt.
No one could find enough to eat.
But in Egypt, Joseph had saved grain
in huge barns.

When Jacob heard this,
he took his family to Egypt to get food.
How glad he was to find his son Joseph alive!

Genesis 42–47

Escape to freedom!

So Joseph's family settled in Egypt.
They were called Hebrews
and kept growing in number.
Years later, a new Pharaoh
made the Hebrews work as slaves.

He was scared that there were too many Hebrews. "Kill every Hebrew baby boy!" he ordered.

25

But one Hebrew mother
hid her baby, Moses, in a basket.
Pharaoh's daughter, the princess of Egypt,
found the basket floating in the river.
Moses was safe!

Exodus 2:1–11

So the princess took the young boy to her palace.
He was brought up as a royal prince.

When Moses grew up, he ran away from Egypt
and went to live in the desert.
One day, an angel spoke to him
from a burning bush.
"Go and tell Pharaoh,
'Let my people go!'."

Exodus 3

28

Moses was scared.
But he went to Pharaoh
many times, saying,
"Let my people go!"
At last Pharaoh gave in.
"Go—and take all
your people with you!"
Exodus 10:21–29

29

Quickly, the Hebrews prepared to leave.
They set out for the land
God had promised them.

Exodus 12:31–39

Pharaoh chased after the Hebrews.
But when he came to the Red Sea,
Pharaoh and all his soldiers drowned.
God saved Moses and his people again!
Exodus 14

The Hebrews stayed in the desert for many years.
God gave them special food called manna.
But they often grumbled and moaned.
They even made a gold statue and danced around it!

Exodus 16, 32

One day, Moses climbed a high mountain.
He came down
carrying two great stones.
On them were God's
rules for everyone.
We call them the
Ten Commandments.
Exodus 20

33

God told his people to build a really big tent,
where the priests could pray to God.
When they moved on, they folded up the tent
and took it with them.

Exodus 26

Into the Promised Land

As they got nearer to the Promised Land,
Moses sent spies to explore.
Two came back saying,
"It's a land full of fruit and good food."

Numbers 13

After many years, Moses died.
God's people crossed the River Jordan.
They entered the Promised Land,
but they still had to capture it.

Joshua 3–4

37

God gave orders for attacking the city of Jericho.
The people walked around and around it.
When the trumpets blew and the people shouted,
the walls fell down!

Joshua 5:13–6:27

God gave his people special new leaders.
One great leader was named Gideon.

Judges 6

With God's help, Gideon beat Israel's enemies.
He attacked at night,
with flaming torches and lots of noise!
The enemy ran away terrified.

Judges 7

At harvest time, the people had a great festival.
They thanked God for all the fruits and grain
in the Promised Land.

Leviticus 23

41

But the people were not happy.
"Give us a king!" they demanded.
"Everyone else has a king."

1 Samuel 8

42

Kings and prophets

So God told his prophet, Samuel,
where to find a man
fit to be king of Israel.

His name was Saul.
Samuel poured oil on Saul's head.
This showed everyone that
God had chosen
him to become king.

At first Saul ruled well.
He led his armies
against many enemies.
1 Samuel 14:15–23

But later, Saul disobeyed God.
So God sent Samuel
to find a new king.

1 Samuel 15

Samuel found a boy
looking after his father's sheep.
His name was David.
Samuel knew God had chosen him
to become the next the king of Israel.

David was brave.
He killed the giant Goliath
with his sling.
The people sang,
"How brave David is!"

Samuel 17

David became a great king.
He loved to play his harp
and sing of God's love.

David made Jerusalem his chief city.

Samuel 5

51

David brought the special box containing
the Ten Commandments to Jerusalem.
He sang and danced in front of it.

2 Samuel 6

When David died, his son
Solomon became king.
Solomon was very wise.

Kings 2

53

When people had problems,
they came to Solomon
to ask him what they should do.

1 Kings 3

The Queen of Sheba lived far away.
She journeyed for days
to hear Solomon's wise words.

1 Kings 10:1–13

55

King Solomon built a beautiful
new temple in Jerusalem.
It was made of the best
gold, wood, and stone.

1 Kings 6

56

The people disobey God

After Solomon died, the people
disobeyed God's laws.
The kingdom was split in two:
one part was called Judah,
the other Israel.

God sent special messengers called prophets.
They told the people to return to God's way.
The prophet Elijah warned wicked king Ahab.

"Worship the living God," said Elijah.
When he prayed
God sent down fire from heaven

1 Kings 17–1

60

God sent many other prophets.
Jeremiah warned there would be war
if the people did not turn back to God.

God sent other prophets.
He sent Isaiah, Daniel, Jonah, and a shepherd named Am

They warned the Israelites,
"Mend your ways,
or God will send
enemies to
defeat you."

63

But still they didn't listen
So cruel kings came and took
the Israelites away to be slaves
They burned the beautiful
city of Jerusalem

2 Kings 2

64

ut the prophets had words of hope, too.
"God still loves you," they said.
"He will send a special person,"
promised the prophets.
"He will save us."

Many years later that special person came,
just as God promised.
His name was Jesus.

Luke 4:14–21

The story of Jesus

Prophets said a special baby
would be born in the
little town of Bethlehem.

Isaiah 7:1

68

He would be called
the Prince of Peace.

69

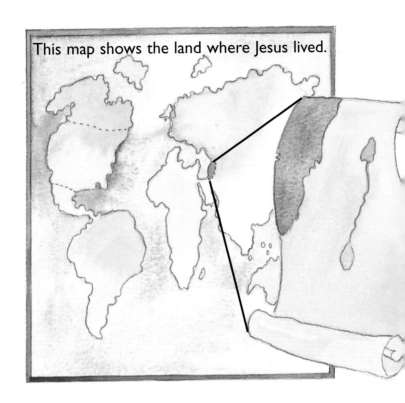

This map shows the land where Jesus lived.

70

The first Christmas

In a town called Nazareth
there lived a young woman named Mary.

One day an angel appeared to Mary.
"You will give birth
to a very special baby,"
he said.
"You must call
the baby Jesus."

Luke 1:26–38

73

Mary went to tell her cousin Elizabeth.
Elizabeth was expecting a baby too.
His name was to be John.
Both women were overjoyed.

Luke 1:39–45

74

Mary married a carpenter named Joseph.
They had to make a long journey to Bethlehem.
Mary was very tired when they arrived.

Luke 2:1–7

75

They could find nowhere to sleep.

An innkeeper said,
"You can stay in my stable."
Mary and Joseph took it gladly.

77

That night some shepherds
were sleeping in fields
near Bethlehem.

Suddenly they saw a bright light.
An angel appeared and said,
"Tonight a child is born in Bethlehem.
He has come to save his people."

78

The shepherds rushed off at once
to find the newborn baby.

Luke 2:8–20

Far away, some wise men saw a special star in the sky.
They decided to follow the star
to find the newborn baby.
They took with them gifts:
gold, frankincense, and myrrh.

At last the wise men came
to the little town of Bethlehem,
where the star shone down.

81

When they saw baby Jesus
they knelt down to worship him

Matthew 2:1–1.

Jesus grows up

Mary and Joseph took Jesus back
to their home in Nazareth.

Here Jesus grew up.
He helped his parents
and played with his friends.

Matthew 2:19–23

When Jesus was twelve,
he went to Jerusalem with his parents
for a special holiday.
But Mary and Joseph lost him in the crowds.

At last they found Jesus again.
He was talking to the Jewish lawyers
in the Temple.
They were astonished
at the wise things he said.

Luke 2:41–52

When Jesus grew up
he worked with Joseph
as a carpenter.
But he knew God
had a special job
for him to do.

88

Jesus' special work

Jesus' cousin, John, started to preach
beside the River Jordan.

He told people to turn away
from the bad things they were doing.

90

He dipped them into the river
to show they were making a clean start.

Matthew 3:1–12

91

Jesus came to the river and asked John to baptize him. The Holy Spirit came down like a dove.

This was the beginning
of Jesus' special work,
the work God wanted
him to do.

Luke 3:1–22

93

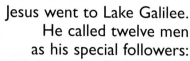

Jesus went to Lake Galilee.
He called twelve men
as his special followers:
Simon Peter
and his brother
Andrew; James
and his brother
John; Philip,
Bartholomew,
Matthew
the tax-man,
Thomas
the twin,
another James,
Simon,
Judas and
Judas Iscariot.

Mark 1:14–20, 3:13–19

95

Jesus taught his disciples
how to pray:
Our Father in heaven:
Holy is your name;
May your kingdom come;
May your will
be done here on earth
just as it is in heaven.
Give us today
the food we need.
Forgive us the wrongs
we have done,
as we forgive those
who have wronged us.
Do not bring us
to hard testing,
but keep us safe
from evil.
Amen.

Matthew 6:9–15

Jesus began to travel
to nearby towns and villages.

He told people special stories
about how God wants our world to be.
People were amazed
when they heard him speak.

Jesus loved children.
He said we should never harm them.

Luke 18:15–17

He wanted people
to love one another.
He said:
"You should always
forgive each other."

Luke 17:3–4

101

Many sick people came to Jesus.
People with bad backs and bad legs.
People who couldn't see and couldn't hear.

Jesus healed them all.

Jesus did special miracles.
One time he fed 5,000 people
with just five loaves and two fish!

Luke 9:10–17

104

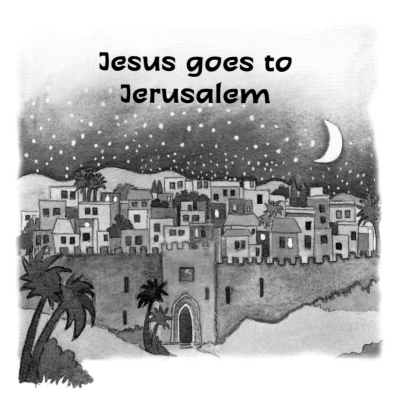

Jesus goes to Jerusalem

Jesus loved Jerusalem.
It was a beautiful city.

106

He decided to travel there again.
Jesus told his disciples,
"I am soon going to die."
They did not understand.

Luke 18:31–34

Some of the people in Jerusalem hated Jesus.
"He doesn't keep our laws," they said.
So they plotted against him.

Judas, one of Jesus' own followers,
turned against him.
He made a plot with Jesus' enemies.
Luke 22:1–6

Jesus arrived in Jerusalem at festival time.
There he borrowed a donkey to ride into the city.

When the people saw him coming,
they waved palm branches.
"Jesus is our King!" they shouted.

Luke 19:28–38

One night Jesus ate a special supper
with his disciples.
Again he said, "I'm going to die soon."
They didn't understand why he said this.

Jesus took bread and poured wine.
"Each time you eat bread or drink wine,"
he said, "remember me."

Luke 22:14–20

Then Jesus and his disciples went out to a garden.
Jesus prayed to his heavenly father.
The disciples fell asleep.

Luke 22:39–46

114

The first Easter

While they were in the garden,
Judas brought Jesus' enemies. Jesus' disciples ran away.

Soldiers took Jesus to the Roman ruler.
He said, "This man has done nothing wrong!"

But the people shouted,
"Kill him! Kill him!"

Luke 22:47–53, 22:66–23:25

118

So soldiers took Jesus away.
They put him to death
on a wooden cross.

Luke 23:26–46

119

Jesus' friends were very sad.
They had lost a special person.

They put Jesus' body in a cave
and rolled a huge stone across the door.
Luke 23:50–56

When they went back to the tomb they saw two angels
inside. The angels said "Don't be afraid! Jesus is alive!
Go and meet him in Galilee."

122

Jesus is alive!

Peter and John
ran to Jesus' tomb.
The stone was rolled away.
They were astonished!

John 20:1–9

124

Soon afterward,
the disciples went fishing.
They saw Jesus on the beach.

125

Peter was so pleased to see Jesus again
that he jumped into the water
and rushed ashore.

John 21:1–14

Not long after this, Jesus left them.
He returned to his Heavenly Father.
But the disciples knew he was alive forever.

Luke 24:50–53

And Jesus promised: "One day I will return as king!"